LOVERS
LUNATICS
&
LALLANG

BY

CECIL RAJENDRA

Published by Bogle-L'Ouverture Publications
141 Coldershaw Road, Ealing, London W13 9DU

First Published in 1989 by:
Bogle-L'Ouverture Publications Ltd.
141 Coldershaw Road
Ealing, London W.13 9DU
England

Distributed by:
Friends of Artistes Liaison, Penang, Malaysia
Bogle L'Ouverture Publications Ltd., London, England

ISBN 0 904 521 47 8

Printed by Practical Printers Sdn. Bhd.
7 Jelutong Avenue, 11600 Penang, Malaysia.

Cover Painting by Yuen Chee Ling

The lunatic, the lover and the poet
Are of imagination all compact.

– SHAKESPEARE –

Other titles by the author:

Embryo
Eros & Ashes
Bones & Feathers
Refugees & Other Despairs
Hour of Assassins
Postscripts
Songs for the Unsung
Child of the Sun
Dove on Fire

CONTENTS

There is always some madness in love.
But there is also always some reason in madness.

– **NIETZCHE** –

MALAYSIAN LOVE SONG

(Adapted from Welsh Love Letter *by* Michael Burn)

Were all the hills in Malaysia
in one huge mountain piled

Muntahak on Tangga
Chintawasa, Chanah
And Tahan on top
And all between us
I'd climb them climb them
All!
To reach you
O, how I love you!

Were all the streams of Malaysia
In one great river joined
Kemaman, Kurau
Temengor, Tembeling
And the Nenggiri in flood
And all between us
I'd swim them swim them
All!
To reach you
O, how I love you!

Were all the kampongs in Malaysia
In one great village linked
Merchong and Mengkarak
Kelujong, Kenanga
Senangar, Senggora
And all in flames
I'd jump them jump them
All!
To reach you
O, how I love you!

p.s. See you Saturday
If there's no football!

MORNING FRAGRANCE

And if
the day's
demands
would effect
upon your
fragile features
an air
of weariness.....

Always too
i scent
about you
a redolence
of freshness.....

a freshness
not so much
of that
cliched daisy
or of some
time-worn flower.....

but more
a freshness
of that attar
of skin of earth
after
a nightfall's
gentle shower.

NOON HEAT

Lungs on fire
  with sanddust

head bursting
  with noonlight

sweat breaking
  off your back...

You squint down
  flambeausun-

slashed streets
  grope towards

the chinasilk-softness
  of an evening

the conchcoolness
  of a woman's thighs.

SALVAGE

Whizzing
    papers
documents
    briefs
affidavits
    letters.....

Hurtling
    careening
into that
    everyday
abyss
    of
        fast-
idious
    nonsense.....

Sanity
    saved
only
    your cameo
i always
    carry
in my
    pouch
    of remembrance.

HINE-RUHI

when you, my Hine-ruhi*
took unconditional flight
that monday morning
turning, turning all
my days into night
at last i knew why
we call our mondays black

once you were gone
out, out went the light
leaving no one
to tempt another dawn
from the horizon
to end my endless night

* *In Maori legend, Hine-ruhi was the woman whose beauty caused the wonder of dawn to reappear.*

CLOUDS

What will I do
now you are gone?
Who can I talk to?

Who will fill the crater
left by your departure?
Who will fire the poems?

Whose smile will wash
away my everyday despair?
And on whose laughter
can i ride again to Hope?

These questions impinge
and the memories.....
as he drives past
that coffee-house where
they last took tea.

And suddenly the streets
are shawled in darkness.
The windscreen films over.
Has it started raining?

He reaches forward
switches on the wiper
quickly switches off;
The sun's still blazing.

And there are
no clouds in the sky.....

Quietly he dabs his eyes.

EXORCISM

Now that you're gone
filaments of laughter
smile and gesture
like hermit crabs
scuttle into my bone.

What I cannot tame
i must exorcise
from the marrow;
turning into my pillow
i call & call your name.....

SLEEPING OUT

Allergic to your absence
i break into an eczema
        of loneliness

Unwelcome guest, Remembrance,
hangs about the verandah
        of melancholy

Desire, unsolicited, mushrooms
in that dank closet of
        concupiscence

while welcome sleep nuzzles
the window-pane unable
        to come in

Under a foreign blanket, i
    itch & toss. Where's
        the amytal?

THE PUMP

You see, it really is a pump
Complex, but extremely efficient
This is the left ventricle
This is the right
And here is the aorta
Veins bring the blood in
Arteries take it out
To lung, brains, et cetera
All very mechanical
Nothing to get emotional about

A system of valves and chambers
And seventy-two contractions
Clenching away per minute
In a normal person
(If you are a normal person)

You see, it really is a pump
Not entirely indispensable
For should it go erratic
From age or over-exertion
One can always replace it
With a Dr. Barnard special
If one has the money
The good man has his scalpel

Yes, it really is a pump
Valve and ventricle
And seventy-two contractions
Systole and diastole
Alternating in orderly fashion
A question of simple
Propulsion rather than emotion

And yet, and yet.....
Why do you do cartwheels
At her footfall in the corridor?
And why do you ache so
Each time she gets up to go?
You stupid pump, you!

LOVE BYTE

Brought together
by a data computer

their elemental passion
was essentially silicon.

Though printouts said
Ram & Rom were made

for each other, grit
in the integrated circuit

caused a short-out.
He was a mean lout

looking for a cheap fling
but she was no flighty thing

who would be anyone's playmate
without a marriage certificate.

And so, this micron conjunction
fizzled out in half a nanosecond.

RECESSION BLUES

It's bad bad news
week in week out.....
factories are a-closing
workers out picketing
but never mind darling
you put your left foot in
you put your right foot out
take your lay-off ticket
and stamp it all about
we'll do the recession blues.

It's bad bad news
month in month out.....
money is a-shrinking
prices are a-soaring
but never mind darling
you put your right hand in
you put your left hand out
take your devalued dollar
and wave it all about
we'll do the recession blues.

It's bad bad news
year in year out
the birth-rate's dropping
everyone's stopped loving
but never mind darling
you put your left hip in
you put your right hip out
take your prophylactic
and shake it all about
we'll do the recession blues.

21ST. ANNIVERSARY

Resurrecting the years. Remembering
ecstasy, laughter & tears. Ferrying
back evergreen days of wine and
eros. Cranking up again that grand
combustion engine of desire.....
can we, some magic yet recapture
after so many trials of ice & fire?

Refuse, refuse to let habit or season
amputate the hours of passion;
jasmine can still bloom in the late
evening of your days. Those who await
nightfall need harbour no fear;
dreams, like safaris, are often sweeter
round tracks at once strange & familiar;
all journeys are determined by the traveller.

REPEATS

Decades have not staled
nor familiarity tethered
the stallions of passion.

i would again asseverate
those vows i once made
when we were young, reckless
& love was full of unreason;

but celluloid has cliched
frozen on feckless tongue
my every would-be declaration.

A LYRIC LIFE
(for Rebecca)

Come let us away
from this prosaic drudgery
my love, let us away
& live in a house of poetry.

It will be an idyll...
We'll have limericks for break-
fast; dactyls for tea. I'll
dress you in finest madrigal.

With sestets on your fingers
and stanzas in your hair
we'll dine on roast couplets
with a flagon of bucolic.

We'll take regular iambic
cantos in the country
with a little doggerel
that's triolet-trained.

I'll pitch a pentameter
in a pastoral roundelay
lay a blank verse
by a running sonnet...

And there, my love
scanning your see-
through metaphor away,
spondee in trochee,

distich in poesy,
we'll rhyme and alliterate
and lyrically aspirate
all the livelong georgic day.

SPACE INVADERS

Loving and lovable
trying/temperamental
irrepressible/irascible
but always adorable.....

who are these monsters .
who often drive us
to the gate of asylums
with their tantrums?

Who turn our bedrooms
into battlefields strewn
with blankets & toys
but who also transmute
the dross of afternoons
into Le Carre thrillers
with stratagems & ploys.

Who can resurrect jaded eyes
to the wonders of a sunflower;
take us on a trip
to the stars with their
bubbly tales and laughter
then plummet us into a pit
of anxiety with a rising fever.

Loving and lovable
trying/temperamental
irrepressible/irascible
but always adorable
these space invaders
we call — CHILDREN!

A politician is an acrobat. He keeps his
balance by saying the opposite of what he does.

– MAURICE BARRES –

We are all born mad. Some remain so.

– SAMUEL BECKETT –

HEADLINES

On newstands
    everywhere
        words·slash
           across our
               morning page

Not jacaranda
    rose or chempaka
        but bayonets, guns
           bullets, fire, rage....

Reminding one
    It's the hour
        of the soldier
           not poet or sage

In this our
    worm-riddled
        doom-destined
           bloodthirsty age.

FOSSILS

We strut about, inflate
our sense of self-importance
we, grist of history
who anthropologists eons hence
may discover, if lucky, as
fossils between sheets of slate!

OUR FUTURE

Our future
lies
before us
in sheets
of White Paper.

After this
5-Year Plan
there will
be another
then another.

There are
no surprises
any more;
only promises...
....
and disappointments!

NOW, SERIOUSLY......

Last year alone
we held twenty-
three seminars
eleven conferences
conducted forty-
seven-point-two
in-depth surveys
appointed sixty-
eight-point-five
research officers
invited thirteen
foreign experts
set up eighteen
special commissions
published sixteen
analytical reports
and issued three
hundred and forty-four
press statements.....
Now, who says we're not·
Serious about restructuring society
Redressing the imbalance
Between haves and have-nots
And forthwith eradicating poverty?

CO-PROSPERITY

Packed tight like coconuts
    in a bullock cart
our heads bob and jerk as
    the overcrowded bus
shoulders her belligerent way past
    trishas, cycles, Hondas
on pinched streets, ferrying us
    to separate destinations.

Clinging to straps, choking on
    fumes of carbon
monoxide, cheap talcum & perspiration
    i begin to wonder
where this motley sweat-sopped clan
    of students, labourers
housewives, secretaries, clerks et cetera
    dovetail into that much-
touted grand new co-prosperity plan?

TOURIST TREAT OR TRICK?

The restaurant left
nothing to chance;
promised not just
the best in local
food and wine
but the 'cream' also
of their traditional
song, music and dance.

At the appointed hour
air-conditioned coaches
and taxis arrived to
disgorge their cargo
of tourist-diners eager
to sample this exotic
feast of cuisine & culture.

Halfway through dinner
to the raucous fanfare
of castanets and congas
they spilled onstage
the singers and dancers
with serviette smiles
as beguiling as their
garlands of plastic flowers.
Singing and screeching
their swivelling hips
in mock-raffia skirts
served a dish specially
concocted for tourists;
neither Asian nor Polynesian
it was cultural desecration
that turned all the wine
in our glasses into vinegar!

IDEOLOGIES

Placed so much higher
on the Government's agenda
than feeding their people
is their military schedule
for crushing erstwhile rebels.

Meanwhile, those "champions
of the people" fighting, they
swear, for peoples' freedom
blow up precious foodtrucks
destined for starving children.

These insanities can only
be reconciled in our world
of poker-player politicians
who deal in bluff, not people.

DEMOCRACY/CAPITALISM/LIBERALISM
MARXISM/SOCIALISM/COMMUNISM
Which brand will the Kremlin buy?
Which label sells best in Washington?

In my mind's eye
i see a child curling
up in the sun to die;
under her tent of skin
her brittle bones creak;

       before dying, i wonder
       what mad ideology
       did those bones speak?

THE ROCK
(for Nelson Mandela)

Thinking you would break
they banished you
to a rock where breaking
stones was all your
trade for over two decades.

In their frenetic scramble
to discredit you
your cause and your struggle
those stone-age
boors left no stone unturned.

But you, Mandela, touchstone
of your people
proved far more durable
than any diamond.
As all around us we witness
apartheid in tatters
we know history will chalk you
the Rock
on which a Republic of Racism
foundered!

ANGELS

History will record
that among us
walked certain angels

whose wings
wove patterns
of laughter
in the air

whose songs
salted
the humdrum
of our days

whose dance
lifted us
made our
lives lighter

History will record
we dismissed
them as cranks
eccentrics, jokers...
all those angels
who walked among us.

DEATH OF THE DANCING FLOWERS

There will be
no more
golden showers
on this lane
anymore.....

The regal angsanas
that rained
their delicate
yellow flowers
have been
scythed down
to make way
for the new
six-lane motorway.

As ever, nature
and beauty
are sacrificed
on the altar
of development
and expediency.

Picking up two
of these tutu-
shaped blooms
my four year-
old daughter
asks in wide-
eyed wonder
if it's true
that there'll
be no more
dancing flowers
on our road anymore.

BITTER SUNSET

And now, our sunsets are
even more magnificent.....

The gold and russet of old
is streaked with silver grey
ochre/magenta/cobalt/crimson
and such a kaleidoscope of
shades and nuances we cannot
find in any artist's lexicon.

Sadly, this splendiferous
eye-feast is cloyed with
bitterness. The wondrous
amalgam of light and colour
is not only God's creation
but product also of man's
purblind unthinking pollution!

WORLD WAR II – THE REAL STORY

And the so-called
rape of Nanking
never happened;
the unfortunate lady
in the documentary
with half-severed neck
did, in actual fact
try to decapitate
herself to make
the Japanese look bad.

And the River Kwai
was a lie
manufactured in
Hollywood
so's Alec Guinness
could win an Oscar!

For the noble Japs
were never aggressors.....
Pearl Harbour, in fact
was bombed by a Jew
who framed the sons
of the Rising Sun
to drag the Yank-
ees into World War Two.

And the Philippines
Burma, Malaya
Singapore et cetera
were never taken by
the Imperial Army.

They were, in fact
Japanese prefectures
occupied by illegal
dark-skinned immigrants
who the brave Tojo
was trying to flush out
in the name of Hirohito!

And, of course
the so-called Holocaust
never did happen.
Six million Jews
locked themselves into
concentration camps
stuffed their bodies into
so-called gas-ovens
and immolated themselves
merely as a publicity
stunt designed solely
to gain them sympathy
and give the poor pure
Aryan race a bad name!

For Hitler was, in fact
a peace-loving pacifist
who adored old ladies
and little children;
as were his comrades
the much misunderstood
General Tojo and Mussolini
all of whom were martyrs
innocently slaughtered for
being conscientious objectors!

For, truth to tell, the Second
World War never did happen;
the so-called World War Two

was no more than
advertisement hype
a puffed-up title con-
jured by boxing promoters
to boost flagging
ticket sales for the return
heavyweight bout between
Joe Louis and Max Schmeling!

BUT STILL THE GOVERNMENT

"*All Singapore-registered vehicles leaving for West Malaysia must have their fuel tanks filled to more than half the capacity the Government announced today. Motorists driving vehicles with fuel gauges showing less than half full, shall be guilty of an offence and shall be liable, on conviction, to a fine not exceeding $500/-.*

— BERNAMA —

But still the Government
suspected their Treasury
of being diddled by
their dollar-wise citizenry.

So they passed another
edict banning all members
of the feminine gender
leaving in mini-skirts;

fearful that that sex
once abroad would deprive
the Republic of fabric tax
by converting them to maxis.

But still the Government.....

So there was another decree
compelling every citizen
planning an overseas holiday
to first be completely shaven;

this was done to ensure
that revenue that might be
spent on a foreign tonsure
remained in the country.

But still the Government.....

35

Thus, a bill was passed
restraining all passport-holders
with half-filled bellies
from slipping across borders;

unnerved that connoiseurs
of exotic alien cuisine
might deplete its coffers
by foreign wining & dining.

But still the Government.....

So yet another law was passed
prohibiting each male citizen
from stepping off the island
without a Cert. of Circumcision;

this guaranteed conservation
of all foreskins, ancillary
medical and sacral taxation
in the Republic's Treasury.

But still the Government.....

THE TREACHERY OF RED

Senior military officer Zhang Gong told TV viewers that not one shot was fired and not a single student had died when the army cleared the square, implicitly denying eyewitness accounts of youths being gunned down or crushed to death under tanks.

– REUTER –

i was not there
in Tiananmen Square
when they danced round
the Goddess of Liberty.

so, who am i
to disagree
with a General
whose word is Gospel.

The man said not
one shot was fired
no one was injured
much less massacred.

Surely there must be some
rational explanation
for all those television
images bombarding our homes:

of claret-splattered shirts
of pools of viscous vermillion
of twisted terror-filled faces
of carmine-streaked children.

Yet, what dumb explication
for such a riot of redness
when students ran screaming
from guns that were silent.

Did the stones ooze ketchup?
Did the Goddess spit chilly?
When tanks rumbled through
leaving magenta gobs of jelly.

The night i was not there
in Tiananmen Square
when they danced round
round the Goddess of Liberty.

THE ROWDY CANDLE

(for Ines Meichsner)

Ines Meichsner, a 20-year old bookbinder was arrested in Dresden while demonstrating with a lighted candle. A search of her house later revealed placards bearing slogans including "Flowers not Bombs", "Make Love not War" and "Live Differently — Disarm". Leaflets carrying an appeal to parents not to buy 'war toys' for their children were also found.

Her indictment alleged her activities constituted "a gross annoyance to the public."

She was charged with "rowdiness" under Article 215 of the GDR Constitution and sentenced to 10 months imprisonment.

— **AMNESTY INTERNATIONAL NEWSLETTER** —

So, you thought
you could get away
with it, eh Ines?
Campaigning for a better
world — a world
of flowers and trees
a world without war.....

No, Ines, the moment
they picked you up
by your burning candle
you were guilty on all counts.

How to plead innocence
when the evidence
piled against you
was so incriminating:
placards with
subversive slogans screaming:
"Flowers not Bombs"

"Make Love not War"

"Live Differently — Disarm".

And what about those
treasonable leaves urging
mothers not to buy
war toys for their children?

Did you really think
you could get
away with it, eh Ines?

In a world of unreason
where 'reasonable' men
hack historic forests
to boost their GNP,
stockpile megabombs
in the name of security,
you were GUILTY
beyond all reasonable doubt.

In a world of darkness
lighting a candle
is the ultimate
act of rowdiness.
And you, dear Ines
by trying to bring
peace and light to
our medieval madness
were guilty of committing
the grossest public annoyance.

So, you thought
you could get away
with it, eh Ines?
Campaigning for a better
world — a world
of flowers and trees
a world without war.....

THE PLEASURE-PAIN SUTRAS

In the Ananga Ranga
(the Hindu Art of Love)
by the poet Kalyana Malla
under sitting positions
is the Kaurmak-asana

or the 'tortoise posture'
where mouth, arms and legs
of the couple are in full
contact with each other;
another is the Gajasawa

or the 'elephant posture'
where the wife is set
in such a position that
face, breasts, thighs etc.
all touch the bed or carpet;
whereupon her husband
extends himself upon her
and bending like an elephant
works to effect an insertion.

The Perfumed Garden lists
29 manners of coition.
There's the second manner:
El modefada - frog fashion;
the fourth manner: El Mokeur-
meutt - with legs in the air;
the fifteenth manner: Dok
el arz — pounding on the spot;
the twentieth manner: Dok
el outed — driving the pin in;
up to the ultimate manner
El moheundi — or, 'the seducer'.

Then, the Kama Sutra
of Vatsyayana catalogues
64 ways of sexual congress
how to touch and pierce
scratch, rub and press;
also, how to shampoo.
The lotus-like position
and the yawning position
and the position known
as 'splitting of a bamboo'.
The embrace of jaghana

and Jataveshtitaka
and the tight embrace
of sesamum seed and rice
called the Tila-Tandulaka.

Yet, though each classic
neatly lists position
procedure and technique
in none will you find a
method known as banera:
where the head is held under
water to point of suffocation;
or pileta: where the head

is plunged into a tank of
water polluted with excrement.

In the Kama Sutra
you will not find feto:
where the female is forced
to remain hour upon hour
in a foetal position;
nor is there chancho:
where the male supported
only by his head
and the tips of his toes
is compelled to lie
parallel with the floor.

In the Ananga Ranga
there is no posture
called pau de arara:
the 'parrot's perch' where
the beloved is suspended
from a rod or axle
placed under the knees
while her hands are
shackled to her ankles.

No listing of la parrilla
la pita, secadera or
falaqa: sustained pounding
of the soles of one's feet;
nor of picana electrica:
where electric shocks are
applied with a cattle prod
to breasts, thighs and vulva.

And in the Perfumed Garden
there is no le rodeo
submarino or telefono.....
nor any mention
of an exotic position
called al-Abd al-Aswad:
where the seated husband
is strapped to an apparatus
which when switched on
inserts a heated metal
skewer right into his anus.

Yes, though the ancient
treatises of our fathers
have so many, many
ways of making love.....
the ways of torture
in the modern manuals
of our latter-day Generals
                    are infinitely more!

THE FINAL WORD

"We must look with caution at the proposition that walling off a portion of the world from nuclear weapons will contribute to peace.

It could instead heighten rather than reduce the risk of war. For this reason we cannot support the proposal for a nuclear-free zone in South-East Asia."

– U.S. President Ronald Reagan –

After
the eagle's
proclamation
a star rose
in the West
and from
four corners
of the earth
doves converged
on the eagle's
White eyrie.....

Not bearing
gifts but with
outstretched
arms pleading:
O Great Wise One
give us nuclear
bombs, missiles
submarines
and satellites
so that we too
may bring peace
in our lands
spread goodwill
to all mankind!

*Politics is the art of preventing people
from taking part in affairs which properly
concern them all.*

— **PAUL VALERY** —

OPERATION LALLANG

Octobering
  our lives
    with fear.....

down
  from Parl-
    iament hill
      an acrid
        wind blows
          sweeping
            this land.

Hither
  and thither
    the lallang
      bends, breaks
        and like
          some hay-
            wire scalpel
              cuts, cuts, cuts.....

Rose, chempaka
  frangipani
    bunga raya
      and all
        the flowers
          of democracy
            bleed.....
              and mothers
              and little
                children weep.

DADDY WON'T BE HOME FOR DINNER

The hour was three o'clock
exactly three in the morning
when rancour rapped the gate
shattered our bubble of sleep
and bundled my husband away
at exactly three in the morning.

We were given no reason
for his arrest, nor information
of where he would be held at.
He spoke for justice, ergo he
was a subversive; in our world
that made him a security threat.

And now the uncertainty
and the not knowing are
twin fists around my throat
strangling our thin hopes:
the not knowing where he is
or how he is, in good health
or bad, hungry or well-fed.

The uncertainty of ever seeing
him again, touching his hand
of sharing his dreams and fears
mapping our children's future;
above all, not knowing how to
tell our little ones this evening
their daddy won't be home for dinner.

CANNED BEAUTY

In a manoeuvre to woo
tourists to this sunny isle
the republic staged a beauty
pageant. Eight and sixty
plastic hopefuls jiggled
down a loudly-lit aisle
to put their vital inches
on trial before a gaggle
of goggle-eyed judges.

Arc-light and camera
bared all to the public:
birth-mark, mole and dimple.
There were no secrets. Media
covered each and every angle
for this Miss Universe winner
would be our Queen for a year.

In a separate operation
to weed out subversives
and keep this island
secure for the tourists
some sixteen others
(not half as glamorous)
were rounded up, herded
down dim-lit corridors
to an uncertain future
beyond the flashing cameras.

Forget their vital statistics...
Save that the sixteen were
involved in dubious politics
little was revealed to the media.

There were no charges, no trial
no judges; for the only winners
of this clandestine operation
were the screws of repression.

INSIDE THE NIGHTMARE

Those on the inside
are always outside —
outside the terror.
They have spoken
paid the penalty
their ordeal is over
now only the waiting.

But here —
beyond the bars —
always the anticipation
— the nervous glance
over the shoulder;
always the perspiration
— the film of fear
that gloves the palms;
and always, always
that all-seeing giant
arc-light of the sun
probing, unrelenting
beating down, softening
you for the half-
expected midnight
knock on the door....

Those on the outside
are always inside —
inside the nightmare.

DEATH IN THE REGISTRY

In an office
somewhere
in the city
a ledger
is taken down
from a shelf
dusted & opened

A finger
runs down
the names
on the page
hesistates, stops....

A fountain pen
is uncapped
a slide rule
unsheathed
a thick line
is neatly drawn
from left to right:
~~CANCELLED~~
And somewhere
in the country
another voice
is stilled
as another nail
is driven
into that coffin!

FOREIGN INTERFERENCE

His chain hotels are run
by Swiss and Austrians;
And his dairy project
monitored by Australians.

His electronic industry
is controlled by Japanese;
And his canning-factory
advisers are all Chinese.

His begging bowl is filled
with aid from the States;
And his cars are fuelled
by the United Arab Emirates.

From the United Kingdom
he imports his professors
and a dour German
coaches his footballers.

Yet, when one small voice
questions his detentions
with magisterial petulance
he stomps his foot and rants
against foreign interference!

FREEDOM OF THE PRESS & PIZZAS

"There is no freedom of the press in the West. The only free press is in Malaysia."

– Datuk Seri Dr. Mahathir Mohamad –

After the P.M.'s pronouncement
that true press freedom
existed only in his country
angry crowds could be seen
storming a pizza counter
run by employees of a paper
shut down for not playing
footsie with the Home Minister.

The mob of befuddled customers
claimed to have been cheated.

As freedom of the press in
their country was exceptional,
impossible that the newspaper
could have been suspended;
impossible too that reporters
could have been laid off;
ergo, the pressmen could not
have opened a pizza stall
ergo, the pressmen could not
have sold them pizzas at all!

It was all a hallucination;
and now the irate customers
demanded their money back.
No matter how well baked
they were damned if they
were paying good money
for pieces of illusions!

LAND OF PSST
(after the Official Secrets Act)

And so it came to pass
(for everything secret was sacred)
that a great cloud of fear
and darkness enveloped the land.....

Everywhere people stopped talking:
not only in government corridors
but from bus stop, market place,
stock exchange & street corners
all one could catch was
the ominous sound of whispering.

Now there was no distinction
between fact, fiction or rumour:
it was a psst-psst here, a psst-
psst there, a psst-psst everywhere.....
conversation was reduced to a whisper.

And not only people but certain
birds and animals were also
infected by this tumour of fear:

in our courthouse, pigeons
who had often eavesdropped
on sundry government proceedings
fearful of mandatory sentences
immediately stopped their cooing.

And deep in our National Park
tigers who were unwittingly privy
to a discussion between the Minister
of Environment and Minister of Industry
toned their roars down to a whisper.

So, as man nor beast could tell
what was or was not a secret
nothing was ever promulgated
everything was just rumoured.

Yes, it was psst-psst here, psst-
psst there, psst-psst everywhere
for the father of the rumour-
monger is the contriver of secrets!

MARSUPIALS & TRIBUNALS

"It will not be a kangaroo court"

— **Tan Sri Abdul Hamid Omar C.J.**
on the tribunal set up to dismiss
Lord President Tun Salleh Abas —

In the climate
of fear
and uncertainty
over
our nation's future
the list
of would-be emigrants
to Australia
gets longer by the hour.

Meanwhile Down Under,
controversy
rages over the influx
& utility
of the sea of immigrants
from Asia.
UNEMPLOYABLE! snorts an M.P.

Our people are more tolerant
we have
not raised a murmur
against
that horde of pouched
immigrants
who, in the uproar, have
quietly
slipped ashore from Down Under.

On the contrary, hospitable
to a
fault, we have not denied
a single
kangaroo gainful employment.

In our beloved country
marsupials
can now often be seen
occupying
positions of High office
in sundry
Supreme Courts and Tribunals!

TOTAL ECLIPSE

Mark this day: Friday
the Eighteenth day of March
in the Year of our Lord
Nineteen Hundred and Eighty-Eight.

On this day in history
as the moon slowly passed
across the sun, our country
experienced a solar eclipse.

Crowds gathered to watch
as an eerie twilight bathed
this land. But cockerels
soon crowed and restored

everything back to normal.
The sun returned to shine in
all her splendour. The eclipse
was but transient and partial.

Mark this day: Friday
the Eighteenth day of March
in the year of our Lord
Nineteen Hundred and Eighty-Eight.

On this day in history
as amendments swiftly passed
in our Houses of Parliament
there was a greater eclipse.

All the lights went out
on our land's Constitution
and plunged the Judiciary
into a Stygian darkness.

There were no crowds. Only
one cockerel crowed. The rest
was silence, though this
eclipse continues and is total!

LESSONS FROM SNOOKER

Scandal   after   scandal
snaffles the table.
Green has gone
we   are
in the
red.

They've pocketed the lot
with every shot
and covered
all   the
angles.

With nothing to cushion
our loss, we scream
till we're baize
and   blue
in   the
face.

But unfazed, the hustlers
chalked on cue, cry:
'Give   us   a
break,   we
have been
framed!

It's   a   clean   up!   The
pot's disappeared. The
scandals hushed up;
and   all   our
tomorrows
snookered!

SUBVERSIVE SAINT

All the man had
he gave the poor:

offered his home
for their shelter,
his life savings
for their sustenance;

hawked his car
to buy medicine,
opened his library
to their children.

And the Government
dubbed him 'saint';
showered him with
accolades, awards
& countless encomiums.

But alas, his largesse
ran out, and our
man, with nothing
left to give, began
asking awkward questions:

why were the poor, poor?
why no employment?
why no food, shelter?
why no education?
what made them poor?

And now the Government
(not a whit amused)
has branded our 'saint'
a subversive/a troublemaker
and packed him off to prison
to serve an indefinite sentence!

ONCE THERE WAS LAUGHTER

Once there was laughter
and singing and dancing
and our people had only
smiles for each other.....

once there was hope
for a better future
where we would stand
shoulder to shoulder
in a land prosperous & free

Then came those grim-
visaged politicians
who put our money
into their pockets
but barbed wire
fences between races
who cold-storaged
our freedom (in
the name of security)
and subverted our history!

Once there was laughter.....

MUDDIED JUSTICE

Drop
    by
        precious
                drop
it has seeped through :

    the chinks in our conscience
    the lacunae in our vigilance.

    the cracks in our constitution
    caused by roughshod amendments.

    fissures in the floorboards
    of Courthouses split apart
    by pusillanimous decisions.

Drop
    by
        precious
                drop
it has seeped through . . . . .

and now Justice is a puddle
of muddy water in the courtyards
of our Courts where small boys jump
in which both feet and ducks paddle !

NO CHANGE

After so many poems
    protest marches
in so many places
    nothing changes
the bitter wind hisses
    the rain spits
but the caravan of horrors
    rumbles on.....

Politicians still lie:
preaching peace & prosperity
while factories grind out
armaments and poverty.

The media anaesthetizes:
blood & begging-bowl eyes
come in the same package
as Beaujolais & Cardin ties.

And our children still die
in desolate burnt-out places
mown down by bullets
hunger and ravaging diseases.

After so many poems
    protests marches
in so many places
    nothing changes
the bitter wind hisses
    the rain spits
but the caravan of horrors
    rumbles on.....

*I'll say that madness, a certain kind of madness,
often goes hand in hand with poetry.
It would be very difficult for predominantly rational
people to be poets, and perhaps it is just as
difficult for poets to be rational.*

– PABLO NERUDA –

ANOTHER MORNING

The amplified voice
of a muezzin
barks electric
from the majestic
    m
    i
    n
    a
    r
    e
    t
of the State mosque;
snapping the city
from its thicket of sleep.

A circle of fireflies —
the luminous dial
of my bedside clock —
semaphore an eerie 5.30.

What can i devise
to pass this purgatorial
hour before sunrise:
too early for a rehearsal
of morning ablutions
too late for a retrieval
of that broken tendril of dreams.

Outside, the estate air is still
grey with remnants of night;
another dawn awaits release
from the scrag throat of a cockerel.

IMPASSE

The morning sun
explodes on my face
with the vengeance
of an interrogator's
     searchlight

Pinned against my pillow
i'm corralled by the usual
unanswerable questions:

     Who am i? What am
     i doing here? What's the
     bloody point of it all?

Yes, the day with its
full freight of terror
has arrived to meet me

i have little desire to stay
and less desire to leave....

ON THE BRINK

1.   Demons stalk corridors
of home, pub & office
pushing him to seek
the anonymity of streets
nondescript coffeeshops
the dog-eared wilderness
of secondhand bookstalls.....

But there is no escape
If only the acetylene
sun could blowtorch
dissolve and meld this
wretched self forever
into the streets' bitumen.

2.   In the Sahara
of his existence
the distance
between oases
of lucidity
lengthen
each year
in inverse proportion
to their compass
which contracts —
eaten by
the attenuating
sands of insanity.

3.   Besieged
by ghosts
real
and imaginary

the walls
of reason
start crumbling
inwards.....

4.   There are ghouls
everywhere
the phone rings
he recoils.....
which goblin
is on the line?
Roar
of the postman's
Honda
fills him with
terror;
what devil
in the mail
will he deliver?
A door knock
unlocks
a cataract
of cold sweat.
Has he been
found out.....
Have they come
to take him away
in Black Maria
or strait jacket?

5. The mind –
   a cowpat –
   buzzed
   without respite
   by legions
   of bluebottles.

6. The mind –
   a madeleine
   wafer-sliced –
   the edges
   nibbled
   by armies
   of cockroaches.

7. The mind –
   an old crone's
   cupboard
   chockfull
   with trifles –
   ready to burst!

8. The mind
   a hothouse
   where smallest
   prickles
   metamorphose
   into giant cactuses.

9. The accretion
    of a lifetime
    of fears
    piles up & up
    into insur-
    mountable prison
    walls hemming
    the mind in.

10. There is no exit
    from this skin
    this caul of fear
    that itches
    and twitches
    at the slightest
            whisper!

11. There is no hell
    each hour
    my mind turns
    and turns
    on a manganese
    spit of never-
    resolving questions;
    i am my own inferno!

12. Alcohol kills brain
    cells
    doctors caution.....
    Good!

i'll drink & drink
to sear
incinerate this sick
suppurating
maggot-infested mind.

13. As if plusses
equal happiness
they chalked up
his accoutrements:
wife, children
titles, profession.....
dubbed him
one of the chosen.

No account
was taken
of the woodworm
nibbling through
his nervous system.

No ledger kept
of nights keyed
and freighted
with fear
nor of retch-
racked red-
eyed mornings
where he weighed
the temptation
of an easy exit
via razor blade
or gas-oven.

No one saw
that hand
tremble
those afternoons
he tried to
squeeze oblivion
from a bottle.

And there were
no witnesses
when he finally
slithered into
irretrievable madness.....

As if plusses
equal happiness
they chalked up
his accoutrements
dubbed him
one of the chosen.

THE MUSE DEPARTS

The poet i know
is always OUT.
The dreamer
& dream have gone.

In his stead
sits a swivel chair
menaced by clients
an army of files
endless appointments.

No room anywhere
for curlicues of
childhood memories
those conduits now
are ever clogged with
ponderous authorities.

No moments either
for mountain walks
or carefree laughter
with friends & family;
no trail's safe where
an adversary stalks
with pestilential sneer
& murderous intensity.

The phone rings.....
a disembodied voice
responds with a
mechanical answer
but the poet i know
is always OUT
the dream & dreamer
        have gone!

RONDO OF DESPAIR

i.   People say
      'How well you look'
      'Never saw you looking better'
      No shatterer of illusions
      I force a smile and say
      'Thank you'

ii.   Mutilated, I rise
      from the Procrustean
      bed of my profession
      and cowled in sweat
      take my place on
      the podium of Life
      to salute the days
      in their uniform
      of grey
      as they pass
      in clockwork procession

      I do not have
      the stamina of days

iii. In this centrally-
      heated jungle
      where the thermostat
      is always turned up
      where idealism shrivels
      and dreams torrefy
      and hopes explode
      like frail balloons....

If you do not wish
to lose sight
if you do not wish
the sun
and her many minions
to cleave
your charred senses
run, run
into the night
despair
in not a flower
to be
worn on one's sleeve

SWAN SONG

And suddenly one night
confronted by forces
you cannot decipher
you begin to discover
life's awful fragility.

Our future hangs
on a slender filament.

Just one small
swish of a razor
a slight squeeze
on the trigger
a drop of poison.....
and any lunatic
can snip the thread
to ring your final curtain.

ROPE

From

    this

matted

    fibre

of

experience

dear

    Lord

let

    me

    twist

some

    small

rope

    of

survival

THE NEWS FROM GONDWANALAND

Good evening, this is Radio Gondwana
here is the 10 o'clock news......

In our main story tonight, the Ministry
of Defence confirmed a report in the London
Times that several Ministers and members
of the Royal Family had received substantial
bribes & kickbacks in respect of a $100-billion
dollar nuclear arms deal with Great Britain.
The Times was telling the absolute truth,
a Ministry spokesman said, and all skeptics
& rumour-mongers were warned against voicing
their suspicions that the story was fabricated.

In a related development, the Sheikh of Nadir,
at a closing down ceremony of the Home
for Handicapped Children in his State,
castigated the British for not including him
in their list of beneficiaries. It was down-
right unfair, he said, and he felt most
slighted. The Sheikh added he would be
taking retaliatory action by withdrawing his
staff and closing down his casino in London.

Meanwhile, the Minister of Education stated
that he had no quarrels with a University
Staff & Students Association report on the
deteriorating academic standards in the Country.
The Minister added, that due to the Government-
inspired brain drain, the quality of education
offered in Gondwana was deplorable & lamentable.

"I myself" the Minister said, "have
taken the precaution of placing my
children in an Australian University."
The Minister urged his fellow middle-
class countrymen to follow his example.

Elsewhere, the Minister of Tourism unveiled
plans to issue another 15,000 Brothel &
Bordello licences in an all-out drive
to increase tourism in the country.
As local women were reluctant to enter
this time-honoured profession, he said
his Ministry was forced to import 150,000
comfort girls from a neighbouring country.

The Minister warned that if our women
continued to refuse to play their role
in boosting the image of our country abroad,
the Government would have no hesitation
in introducing legislation in Parliament
making it compulsory for all females
between the ages of 15-25 doing National
Service in Government-Gazetted Cathouses.

Meanwhile, the victorious candidate in
the recent bye-election, Senator Fraud
admitted opposition claims that the polls
were rigged. He confirmed that the ruling
party, Fatherland United Coalition (FUC)
had created some 75,000 phantom voters
who were responsible for his landslide win.
The Senator berated the opposition party
for crass stupidity in not following suit.

While still on the bye-election, the Prime
Minister gleefully announced in Parliament
that the unsuccessful opposition party
candidate was being held on charges
of treason. He went on to say that
the candidate would shortly be brought
to trial before a kangaroo tribunal
and thereafter sentenced to death as he
had incurred the displeasure of the King
by defiantly contesting the bye-election.

His Majesty, in his recent birthday
message to the nation, had categorically
urged the people to vote for Fatherland
United Coalition (FUC) whom he believed
should remain in power for eternity.
Those against FUC, the King said, suck!

And now for an item of foreign news.....
We have just received confirmation
that Gondwana's chief drug baron
was, in fact, arrested at Kennedy
International Airport last night while
attempting to smuggle in 100,000 tons
of pure heroin in his private jumbo jet.
The General of Police, when contacted
said that he was horrified at the arrest
of Gondwana's most outstanding citizen.

The General assured the people he
would leave no stone unturned in his
efforts to extradite the drug kingpin
to Gondwana where he would be freed uncon-
ditionally and accorded a hero's welcome.

The General added that he regarded
the arrest as an act of foreign inter-
ference in the internal affairs of our
country and was outraged that Western
governments were still attempting to
impose their imperial, neo-colonial
values and cultures on our people.

Later, receiving a donation of $1.5 million
to the Policemen's Undercounter Fund from an
international drug syndicate, the General
accused Western bloc countries of being
insensitive to indigenous customs
and of being particularly ignorant of
the significant contributions made by drug
traffickers to the economies of the region.
Drug trafficking, he said, was Gondwana's
largest single foreign exchange earner.
He pledged that a giant marble memorial
would shortly be erected in the Capital
to commemorate the invaluable benefits
the drug trade has brought to our society.

Commenting on an Amnesty report on torture,
the Minister of Home Affairs regretted
that the section relating to Gondwana
was so brief and insubstantial. Torture
in the country, the Minister said, was
far more widespread and rampant.

He accused Amnesty of racial discrimination
in devoting only 10 pages in their report
to the use of torture in Gondwanaland.
And, dismissed as propaganda a suggestion
that the use of torture here was in decline.

The Minister assured human rights groups
that torture would continue to be used
under the country's next five-year plan.
A budgetary allocation of $50-million
dollars had already been earmarked
for the purchase of sophisticated electrical
equipment to replace the instruments
of torture currently used in our prisons
and police stations, which the Minister
described as antiquated, primitive and ineffective.

Now, for an item on sports........
In our main story tonight, over 900
past Olympic gold medallists have
signed a declaration admitting the use
of steroids. In a strongly worded
statement the Olympians recommended
that the use of anabolic steroids be made
mandatory in all future competitions.

Meanwhile, the International Olympic
Council has directed all past medal
winners who were not on steroids, to
surrender their medals immediately.
The Council accused them of cheating
and ruled that the medals had been won
illegally as they had competed with an
unfair advantage over chunky fellow
athletes who were bulked down by steroids.

And to end our news bulletin
here is the weather report......
tomorrow, it will be sunny in the Capital
elsewhere it will snow.

Early
morning temperatures in the Arctic are
expected to be in the high Nineties;
At the Equator it will be minus zero!

Here's wishing you all an upside-down week-end....

DEBRIS

So many pictures
of blood-rimmed
eyes and tears
of broken bodies
of promises abrogated
and trampled countries...

As the recitation
of human folly
unfolds nightly
on our news-screens
an oilslick
of despair spreads
to blanket & choke
the waters of hope.

History has taught
us sweet NOTHING.
Like dogs chained
to their own vomit
we return to old inanit-
ies over & over again.
How is one to cope?

And yet, and yet...
even from a debris of dreams
a new sun can rise...

GLOSSARY

chempaka: a sweet smelling orange-tinted flower.

angsana: a large flowering tree frequently grown by roadside for its shade.

la parrilla: the metal grill, consisting of electric shocks to the most sensitive parts of the bodies.

la pita: involves binding or handcuffing hands behind the back; victims are then lifted by their wrists by a rope thrown over a beam while at the same time breathing is obstructed by wet rags placed over the nose and mouth.

secadera: where the victim is wrapped in a plastic sheet and placed in a cylinder.

submarino: near asphyxiation by submersion of the head or upper part of the body in tanks of water.

telefono: the telephone, consisting of blows with the palms of the hands on both ears simultaneously.

le rodeo: the rodeo, in which victims are forced to run or crawl carrying heavy weights until they drop with exhaustion.

Lallang: a wild weed-like tropical grass with razor-shape edges. In October 1987, over 100 educationists, academics, social workers, environmentalists, and politicians, including the Malaysian Parliamentary Leader of the Opposition, were rounded up and detained under the Internal Security Act (detention without trial) in a nation wide sweep known as Operation Lallang. Four national newspapers were also shut down. All the detainees have since been freed.